SUMMARY of Catherine Shanahan, MD's DEEP NUTRITION

Why Your Genes Need Traditional Food

by SUMOREADS

Copyright © 2017 by SUMOREADS. All rights reserved. This book or parts thereof may not be reproduced in any form, stored in any retrieval system, or transmitted in any form by any means—electronic, mechanical, photocopy, recording, or otherwise—without prior written permission of the publisher, except as provided by United States of America copyright law. This is an unofficial summary and is not intended as a substitute or replacement for the original book.

TABLE OF CONTENTS

EXECUTIVE SUMMARY 5

PART I: THE WISDOM OF TRADITION 7

Key Takeaway: Your lifestyle choices determine your health—and that of your children. 7

Key Takeaway: Take on the human diet to unlock your health and genetic potential. 8

Key Takeaway: Your genes learn how to behave from your lifestyle. 8

Key Takeaway: Genetic wealth is the privilege of people who eat diverse, nutrient-dense food. 10

Key Takeaway: Beauty and physical fitness are intricately connected. 11

Key Takeaway: Optimal nutrition makes beautiful, healthy children. 12

PART II: THE DANGERS OF THE MODERN DIET 13

Key Takeaway: Excessive focus on the chemical components of food anticipated the shift from real, traditional foods to fake foods. 13

Key Takeaway: Natural fats are healthy choices; processed fats are what wreak havoc in your body. 14

Key Takeaway: Vegetable oils attack the brain, accelerate its aging, and predispose it to neurologic disorders. 16

Key Takeaway: Excessive sugar disrupts cellular and hormonal functions, accelerates mental decay. 17

PART III: LIVING THE DEEP NUTRITION WAY . 19

Key Takeaway: All healthy traditional diets share four attributes that code DNA for health, intelligence, and beauty. 19

Key Takeaway: Eat foods that send your body the right message to lose weight and keep fit. 21

Key Takeaway: Take bone broth to build your connective tissues and forestall aging. 22

Key Takeaway: Go on the human diet to get optimal nutrition. 23

EDITORIAL REVIEW **25**

ABOUT THE AUTHORS **27**

EXECUTIVE SUMMARY

In their book *Deep Nutrition: Why Your Genes Need Traditional Food*, Catherine and Luke Shanahan explain how genes change their activity based on the chemical information they receive from food and how a diet disconnected from nature has anticipated modern epidemics. Digging through years of research and the latest findings in epigenetics, they illustrate the diet that kept ancient tribes fit and disease-free.

Catherine and Luke Shanahan contend that modern epidemics are not random. Most of the mutations that cause diseases can be traced back to the lifestyle choices that turn genes on and off. Depending on whether they are positive or negative, these changes in gene expression could mean better health outcomes or mark the onset of health complications such as diabetes, cancer, mental disorders, and autoimmune diseases. The modern diet—which is rich in pro-inflammatory processed oils and sugars that send the wrong messages to the body—is responsible for most of these conditions. In the view of the duo, your health, as well as the health, intelligence, and beauty of your children, comes down to what you eat and how much you exercise.

According to the authors, virtually all traditional diets—which are quintessential healthy selections of food—share four attributes that program the body for physical fitness, intelligence, and beauty. They are rich in meat on the bone, fermented and sprouted foods, organs, and fresh plant and animal products. Going on a diet centered on these four pillars not only increases your energy and mental focus, it boosts your vitality and longevity and optimizes your organ function.

PART I:
THE WISDOM OF TRADITION

Key Takeaway: Your lifestyle choices determine your health—and that of your children.

For decades, scientists thought diseases such as cancer and undesirable physical conditions such as knock-knees were caused by fixed genetic mutations. If you had bad genes, nature had simply dealt you a bad card that you had to live with.

Recently, epigenetic researchers have established that the condition and performance of genes depends on the lifestyle choices people make. This new breed of scientists argues that environmental influences have more to do with undesirable physical conditions than genetic influences. People are not necessarily born with bad genes. It is exposure to adverse environmental factors—mostly toxins and nutrient deficiencies—that causes good genes to go rogue.

Human genes are not static; they are programmed to learn and adapt to the chemical information they receive. What you eat and do changes the way your genes function in both desirable and undesirable ways. These genetic changes, which manifest in changes in weight, physical ability, appearance, and disease susceptibility, are passed down to the next generation. Sometimes these changes are magnified in subsequent generations.

"Getting sick isn't random. We get sick because our genes didn't get what they were expecting, one too many times... food can tame unruly genetic behavior far more reliably than biotechnology" (p. 8).

Key Takeaway: Take on the human diet to unlock your health and genetic potential.

Chronic illnesses are the outgrowths of a culture that has strayed from traditional cuisine. The modern diet most Americans are on today is so nutrient-deficient that virtually everyone needs supplements just to meet the daily recommended intake of vitamins and minerals. Worse, the effects of a bad diet are felt generations down the line. Healthy parents who are on a poor diet deny their children a similar potential for health.

The traditional, authentic cuisines that protected and restored heath—and assured generations of beautiful and physically fit children—were founded on four pillars. These nourishing diets were heavy on meat cooked on the bone, organs and offal, raw plant and animal products, and fermented and sprouted foods. Most of the healthiest tribes in the world—from the ancient Egyptians to the Japanese—took these foods every day.

Key Takeaway: Your genes learn how to behave from your lifestyle.

About 98 percent of your DNA sequence is made up of non-coding DNA. This DNA, commonly referred to as "junk

DNA" directs the roles of the cells in your body. If junk DNA turns on the wrong cell type, the wrong quantity of cells, or simply turns on cells at the wrong time, the misdirection can cause cancer or other adverse conditions.

Your body gets the chemical information it uses to turn on genes from the nutrients in the food you consume. Simple nutrients such as vitamins, minerals, and fatty acids influence the tags that control how genes work. When nutrients are deficient, DNA mutates so that the parent and offspring can cope with the deficiency. Essentially, nutrient deficiency forces the body to make compromises and adjust to what is available.

These compromises occur throughout life as genes learn and adapt to the environment they are exposed to. Identical twins in their early years, for example, have similar sets of genes. The expression of these genes differs as they age. This change suggests genes respond to environmental influences, which alter the genetic markers for body structure and intelligence.

A lot of vitamin D and calcium, for example, doesn't just give you stronger bones; it turns on genes for building bones. These turned-on genes are passed on to the offspring, who will also have the potential for strong bones. If you take low amounts of vitamin D and calcium, you get weaker bones, and the genes for building bones remain dormant. These genes can be reactivated by modifying diet because genes are intelligent learners. Followed consistently enough, good nutrition can reprogram faulty genes.

A pro-oxidative, pro-inflammatory environment (such as that created by a diet high in vegetable oils) impairs gene transcription, expression, and maintenance. For example, 4-HNE—a lipid product derived from the oxidation of some processed fats—interacts with DNA and creates compounds that prevent it from copying itself accurately. This leaves the DNA susceptible to environmental toxins and mutations that cause, among other conditions, autism and cancer.

Key Takeaway: Genetic wealth is the privilege of people who eat diverse, nutrient-dense food.

When dentist Weston Price travelled the world in the 1930s in search of superhuman races, he discovered that the people who had the total package—perfect teeth, beauty, spectacular general health, and life expectancy that exceeded a hundred years—were part of primitive tribes who subsisted on native diets. Price noted that people with well-formed features drew their beauty and vitality from the foods they ate, not from random occurrences in nature. Their food had at least ten times more vitamins and as much as fifty times more minerals than that of modern Americans, most of whom suffer symptoms of poor nutrition such as yeast infections and dry skin.

These secluded tribes amassed their genetic wealth from cultural practices that were heavily focused on collecting and concentrating nutrients. The islanders of Melanesia ate virtually every part of their wild-grazed hogs, and the natives of the Scottish Isles stuffed oatmeal and chopped livers into cod's heads, which they baked and ate. The plants they ate grew on regularly replenished mineral-rich soils, unlike today's soils which have been exhausted by continuous commercial exploitation. Each of these tribes had special foods that they used to fortify the mother's diet during the gestation and nursing period.

Key Takeaway: Beauty and physical fitness are intricately connected.

Physical attractiveness says a lot about a person's health and physical ability. "Funny looking kids" are more likely to develop learning and socialization disorders, internal organ malformations, and genetic illnesses than children with ordinary or good looks. Physical asymmetry often interferes with the development of internal and external features to cause a wide range of health issues.

Beyond function, beauty has a significant effect on self-reported measures of well-being. People with good looks are more likely to rate themselves as healthier and happier than their less attractive peers.

While debates over what qualifies as beauty abound, beauty is, at its most basic, the proportionality of facial and bodily features. People derive pleasure from looking at beautiful faces because their dynamic symmetry resonates with the brain's internal symmetry. Part of the reason people are attracted to beautiful faces is because they subconsciously use the symmetry they perceive to predict fitness and good genes.

Optimal nutrition is the prerequisite for the healthy and symmetrical development of the human form. Women with the hourglass figure—the embodiment of the ideal female physique—are rare today because of generations of poor nutrition.

Key Takeaway: Optimal nutrition makes beautiful, healthy children.

A second child may be not be as healthy or as good looking as the first if the mother does not give her body enough time and nutrients to foster the optimal in utero environment. The first baby draws as much of its mother's vitamins and minerals as it can, even when the mother is malnourished. If the space between the first and second birth is less than three years, the second baby may form in a nutrient-deficient environment and grow with significant disadvantages. If the mother is on a poor diet such as one high in sugar and vegetable oils, the same outcome is possible.

Poor nutrition and lifestyle choices (such as smoking) blunt growth signals and contribute to birth defects, weak bones and cartilage, asthma, and other health complications. Synthetic vitamin pills cannot fully offset some of these defects because they don't contain the entire range of nutrient molecules in real food. In their synthetic form, most of the vitamins go unabsorbed. Worse, prenatal pills give mothers a false sense of security—that they can make up for a poor diet with multivitamin pills.

Poor diet predisposes children to biradial (left to right) and dynamic (phi, or the natural golden ratio) asymmetry. Either form of asymmetry affects both looks and health. You can minimize the risk of having chronically sick children by eliminating processed and junk foods from your diet, having children at least three years apart, and taking vitamin-rich foods before conception.

PART II:
THE DANGERS OF THE MODERN DIET

Key Takeaway: Excessive focus on the chemical components of food anticipated the shift from real, traditional foods to fake foods.

Most modern epidemics—from heart attacks and strokes to obesity and allergic reactions—can be traced back to changes in the meaning of food. For centuries, and especially in herder-gatherer tribes such as East Africa's Maasai, food was part of the people's identity. Today, food is only evaluated in caloric and nutritional terms. The intimate, near-religious relationship people had with their land, plants, and animals has long been lost and, with it, the culinary traditions that fostered vitality and longevity.

Over the years, physical anthropologists have found that body size—including bone and brain size—shrank as hunter-gatherers moved away from the food variety in the wild to the limited choices of modern agriculture. This shift in diet also lessened phi-proportionality. Generations of poor diet have changed bone structure and caused dental arch deformities that were unheard of in ancient times.

Marked changes in body size and proportionality began right about the time popular cookbooks began contracting foods into their biochemical properties during the Industrial Revolution. Complex foods became carbohydrates, proteins, and fats. This change in language popularized the deceptive idea that all foods were the same, regardless of their source or level of processing. All the details that mattered to ancient tribes—including the soil plants grew on, the time food was harvested, the health of the animals—became inconsequential minutiae as people disconnected from nature. The new priorities—chief among them convenience and low-cost—trumped concerns over how foods are made, how fresh and nutritious they are, and what flavor they have.

Key Takeaway: Natural fats are healthy choices; processed fats are what wreak havoc in your body.

Conventional dietary advice, which advocates for foods low in fats and cholesterol, is not only unfounded, it negates the value of the traditional, natural fats that mankind has subsisted on for millennia. The low-fat diet was popularized in part by a fame-hungry pseudo-scientist and in part by a legion of profit-seeking margarine producers keen on convincing consumers that hydrogenated vegetable oils were the healthier compromise.

"Those who mean to replace natural, traditional foods with modern-day food-like products in the name of health are championing the position that nature doesn't know best; a corporation does" (p. 122).

Cholesterol and natural, saturated fats such as butter have never been the problem. Industrial fats that do not exist in nature, such as vegetable oils, are the poisons that stiffen arteries and multiply the risk of cardiovascular disease. These fats contain polyunsaturated fatty acids that change into (among other toxic compounds) trans fats when heated and clog arteries with plaque.

Natural fats such as butter, animal fats, coconut oil, olive oil, and any unrefined oil are good for your health. Your body can't adapt to processed fats such as canola oil, sunflower oil, corn oil, and non-butter spreads. These fats change cellular function and precipitate a wide range of health complications, including heart conditions, weight gain, and chronic diseases.

Trans fats and other fats distorted by complex extraction processes are especially bad for you because they use free radicals to mutate normal fatty acids in your body. These free radicals can damage your cell membranes and cause inflammation, which disrupts normal metabolic processes. Worse, vegetable oils increase oxidative stress which disrupts the normal development of a fetus.

Any food rich in vegetable oils damages apoproteins (the proteins that guide fat particles to where they are needed) and, consequently, disrupts the circulation of lipids in the body. When their navigation is damaged, the lipoproteins that transport lipids in the blood are lost, so they collect in artery linings and cause atherosclerosis: the hardening of the arteries. Sugar usually combines with vegetable oils to destroy lipoproteins and exacerbate the damage to the arteries. If lipoproteins pile in the arteries long enough, they fry the arterial walls and make them susceptible to tearing and bleeding. When artery walls rupture, the clots that form block circulation and, consequently, cause heart attack or stroke.

Key Takeaway: Vegetable oils attack the brain, accelerate its aging, and predispose it to neurologic disorders.

Vegetable oil attacks the brain from several fronts to cause childhood neurological disorders, depression, Alzheimer's, and a host of other neurodegenerative disorders.

The first line of attack is the gut. When vegetable oil reaches the stomach, it catalyzes oxidative reactions that cause inflammation. This inflammation manifests in symptoms such as gastritis and heartburn. Usually, it spreads insidiously and without symptoms throughout the rest of the gut. Inflammation not only disrupts gut flora, it makes the gut more permeable to toxins and undermines its ability to absorb nutrients. These disruptions affect immune function, as well as mood, memory, and cognition.

The very nature of vegetable oils, such as their susceptibility to oxidative reactions, makes them slow brain killers. Trans fats interact with and deplete the antioxidants the brain needs to defend itself against the free radical reactions that interfere with its normal function. The immediate symptoms associated with oxidative stress include migraines and seizures. Over the long term, accumulating oxidative stress may lead to Alzheimer's, Parkinson's, multiple sclerosis, and other neurodegenerative disorders. Most of the symptoms of these disorders can be prevented or alleviated by sticking to a diet free of vegetable oils and rich in antioxidants such as vegetables, spices, and herbs.

One of the functions of antioxidants is to protect the nitric oxide that instructs blood vessels to dilate and allow the flow of more glucose, oxygen, and other materials that the brain needs to perform optimally. When the distorted fats in vegetable oils deplete antioxidants, the flow of these materials is lowered. Limited blood and glucose flow cause fatigue and brain cramps that make it difficult to learn or perform difficult tasks.

Key Takeaway: Excessive sugar disrupts cellular and hormonal functions, accelerates mental decay.

When sugar is dissolved, it reacts with the proteins in the body to form sticky chemical bonds. These temporary bonds become permanent bonds when oxidized. When this combination of sugar and proteins accumulates long enough, it hardens cells and tissues, and consequently, prevents nutrients from leaving the bloodstream. The trapped nutrients end up in the arteries where they cause blood clots and prevent white blood cells from leaving the bloodstream and going where there's tissue damage. The consequence is usually joint problems and recurring infections.

Excessive consumption of sugar affects more than your arteries and joints. When blood sugar levels are high, the pancreas produces insulin to get the sugar out of the bloodstream. If these blood sugar levels are persistently high, the cells that clean up the sugar respond slowly to insulin, and blood sugar levels keep rising. Over time, prediabetes and, eventually, diabetes, develops. Fasting blood sugar levels above the normal range (about 100mg/dl) may lead to blindness, kidney failure, stroke, and heart attack, among other complications. Sugar addictions may induce shaking spells, confusion, anxiety, seizures, palpitations, and severe headaches as the hormone and energy surges that sugar induces wreak havoc in the body.

Even more insidious is the effect sugar has in children. Sugar induces a release of endogenous opiates which stimulate the brain. This stimulation interferes with the development of children's arousal and alertness systems—sometimes to the point of making them lethargic—and blunts their coping skills.

High-sugar diets damage dendrites (the branches that exchange chemicals and facilitate cognition and the experience of emotion) and make it harder to learn. A persistent loss of these branches often marks the onset of Alzheimer's dementia.

All variations of sugar—including glucose, fructose, maltose, dextrose, and corn, malt, and maple syrup—have about the same effects in the body. Both simple and complex carbohydrates are basically sugar, because that's what the digestive system converts them into. A healthy diet should limit the amount of carbs to healthy quantities—preferably under 100 grams a day.

Low-fat diets are not necessarily low-calorie because they are usually loaded with sugar to make them palatable.

PART III:
LIVING THE DEEP NUTRITION WAY

Key Takeaway: All healthy traditional diets share four attributes that code DNA for health, intelligence, and beauty.

Interpretations of traditional diets often leave out the four common and time-tested sources of nutrition: meat on the bone, fermented and sprouted foods, organs, and fresh plant and animal products. In the spirit of convenience, modern cookbooks substitute traditional ingredients that are hard to find with locally sourced ingredients and leave out foods that take too long to prepare. By so doing, these cookbooks cut out both nutrients and flavor.

Meat has more flavor and nutrition when it is cooked with the bone, marrow, fat, skin, and its connective tissues. These parts release joint-building molecules (including glucosamine, which rejuvenates the body and reverses injuries and disease) as heat and water pulls them apart.

Even more flavor and nutrients are retained when meat from grass-fed cows is cooked slowly at gentle heating temperatures. When steak is done properly, it should be juicy and red. Pasture-raised meat not only has less of the herbicides and pesticides used to spray fodder—and less of the antibiotics and growth hormones injected into commercially bred animals—, it has more bio-concentrated nutrients because it grazes on nutrient-rich grass.

Offal meats, including the kidney, liver, tongue, and head, have been used for centuries as sources of pregnancy- and life-sustaining vitamins. The liver, which stores excess proteins, minerals, and vitamins, especially works well as a natural supplement. Brain and nervous tissues are rich sources of omega-3, and windpipes have connective tissue compounds that strengthen joints.

When plants ferment or sprout, most of their protective mechanisms—including neurotoxins, allergens, and carcinogens—are deactivated, and their nutrition increases. Seeds moistened for just a few days release their store of fats, proteins, and minerals and create new nutrients as they get ready to germinate. On their part, the good bacteria and fungi—the probiotics—which are obtained from live-cultured foods boost the immune function and prevent allergic and inflammatory diseases.

Eating a variety of fresh greens, herbs, and spices gives you all the antioxidants you need without suffering through the side effects of supplements. Fruits, vegetables, and herbs are most potent when they are fresh because drying and heating ruins their antioxidants. However, you may need to gently cook some greens to break the indigestible cellulose that locks in nutrients.

Fresh, unprocessed milk, especially from cows grazed on pasture, is more nutritious than pasteurized milk. Pasteurization denatures proteins and other nutrients in milk. The risk of disease it eliminates is almost negligible. You can take raw milk or ferment it into cheese to retain the nutrients lost to the process. Use live-cultured products such as sour cream, yogurt, and cottage cheese to recolonize your gut with beneficial bacteria.

Key Takeaway: Eat foods that send your body the right message to lose weight and keep fit.

Whether you gain or lose weight depends more on the chemical information your body gets from your diet and lifestyle than from the calories you consume. Foods with the right message, such as those that make up the human diet, tell your body to grow leaner and healthier. An Omega-3 (from the essential fats in eggs and cold-water fatty fish) and Omega-6 (common in soy, corn, vegetable oils) imbalance, on the other hand, tells your body to lose muscle and store fat.

"Our bodies continue to be a work in progress throughout our lives, every cell in our body guided by what our diet is telling us about the outside environment" (p. 275).

Inflammation blocks cellular communication and sends its own messages that tell the body to store fat. For this reason, any weight loss plan must begin with the elimination of pro-inflammatory foods. Vegetable oils, which generate pro-inflammatory free radicals when heated, are obvious candidates. Eliminate all foods prepared with vegetable oils and stock up on foods with the anti-inflammatory saturated fat such as cream, butter, and coconut oil.

Sugar is also pro-inflammatory because it coats cells and blocks hormone signals. High-fructose corn syrup and other sugars turn on liver enzymes which convert these sugars into fat. Cut back consumption of starchy foods to less than 100 grams a day.

When you take on a diet heavy in starch, trans fat, and sugars and limit your exercise, your body takes it to mean that food is scarce. In response, it turns stem cells into fat cells to maximize fat storage. Stem cells can differentiate into any body tissue, so the right message can signal them to turn to bone, muscle, or blood vessels.

The right message can even turn fat cells into stem cells, and then into other types of cells. Exercise—especially prolonged aerobic exercise that makes you pant and sweat—sends the right signals to fat and stem cells by increasing insulin sensitivity, reducing the stress hormone cortisol, and accelerating the growth of new blood vessels in muscles and tissues. Restricting calories and food volume rarely works for sustainable weight loss because fat cells are never repurposed.

Key Takeaway: Take bone broth to build your connective tissues and forestall aging.

Collagen is the structural protein in your connective tissues that, when healthy and flexible, gives you a youthful look. Collagen proteins don't just keep the skin flexible; they also unite adjacent cells in your bone tissues, brain, lungs, and every organ and gland in your body.

The body makes collagen from collagen-rich organs in your food such as tendons and tripe. It directs the nutrients in bone broth to the parts that need collagen such as weak or fractured bones, joints, and connective tissues. Supplement these nutrients with foods rich in vitamins A, D, E, C, and common minerals to look and feel young and stay fit past retirement age.

Since collagen is sensitive to metabolic imbalances, nutrient-deficient diets—especially those loaded with pro-inflammatory fats and sugar—weaken its integrity and damage it. The consequence is stiff and weak joints, disfigured scars, circulatory problems, wrinkling, and accelerated aging.

Key Takeaway: Go on the human diet to get optimal nutrition.

You can make the transition to the healthier human diet today. Start by cutting back your consumption of carbs, and replace sugary drinks with lemon water or herbal tea. Follow through by eliminating snacks, and replace vegetable oils with natural fats from foods such as butter, cheese, cream, nuts, and eggs. Add nutrients from the human diet to complete your new, healthy lifestyle.

The human diet has four pillars:

• Meat on the bone, including barbequed spare ribs and chicken soup. You can use broth to braise vegetables, make soups, or add it to any meal cooked with water.

• Organ meats, including chicken liver, lamb kidneys, bone marrow, and blood sausage from grass-fed animals. Take these organ meats one to three times a week.

- Fermented and sprouted foods such as yogurt, cheddar cheese, sprouted grain bread, and old-fashioned oat porridge. Beans and grains soaked in water for 1-4 days release and add nutrients to your food.

- Fresh foods such as fresh greens, garlic, sushi, nuts, seeds, and raw dairy products such as raw-milk cheeses.

You'll have more success following through the Human diet if you have a daily plan that includes what to buy and what to cook. Make a plan to shop two to three days a week so you have fresh foods. Settle on a few bases—the main ingredients—for each of your meals and combine them with variations of foods on your plan. Breakfast meat, eggs, and yogurt, for example, are bases that can be combined with nuts, seeds, or vegetables. Schedule foods that take time to prepare for dinner so you don't rush the process or bail out.

It's important to watch your macronutrients because, if you are like most Americans, you are getting too little or too much of some. Limit your carbs to less than 100 grams a day, and schedule carbohydrate-rich foods for dinner. For proteins, aim for between 50 and 150 grams a day. Too little protein reduces the capacity of the antioxidant enzyme, and too much protein makes uric acid which may cause gout, a kind of arthritis. There is no maximum recommended intake for fat. It should account for between 60 and 85 percent of your daily caloric intake. Fat doesn't take up much space on your plate because it is loaded with calories. Two teaspoons of butter, for example, may have as much as 200 calories.

EDITORIAL REVIEW

In their book *Deep Nutrition: Why Your Genes Need Traditional Food*, Catherine and Luke Shanahan argue that traditional foods, embodied in what they term the Four Pillars of traditional cuisine, program human genes for the inheritable qualities of health, beauty, and intelligence. They observe that the Four Pillars of the human diet—meat on the bone, offal, fermented and sprouted foods, and fresh plant and animal products—have provided optimal nutrition to ancient tribes for millennia.

The Shanahans contend that the most common ingredients of the modern diet—vegetable oils and sugar—cause inflammatory reactions that wreak havoc on the gut, bones, brain, and other major organs. On the rising incidence of diseases such as diabetes, heart disease, stroke, erectile dysfunction, and Alzheimer's they note:

"What's been dropping us like flies is not any upsurge in saturated fat consumption, but an upsurge in consumption of two major categories of pro-inflammatory foods: vegetable oils (a.k.a. unnatural fats) and sugar" (p. 129).

The authors deliver these two key messages passionately and in language that anyone can understand. They supplement theory not just with a list of foods to eat and products to avoid, but with comprehensive resources, including a carb- and protein-counting tool and a list of brands that carry healthy products.

What is most remarkable about *Deep Nutrition* is that it offers more than nutrition advice. The authors dedicate nearly a quarter of the book to explaining how ancient tribes enjoyed better health outcomes by eating close to nature, how genes draw from nutrition to code for fitness and beauty, and how mothers unwittingly deny their children a shot at winning the genetic lottery. From Weston Price's adventures in secluded communities to distant travelers' accounts of tribes that had a reverent bond with food, *Deep Nutrition* offers a fascinating anthropological take on the fusion of food and identity.

ABOUT THE AUTHORS

Catherine Shanahan is an American author, a board-certified family physician, and a nutrition consultant for the LA Lakers and Mark Sisson's Primal BluePrint certification program. *Deep Nutrition* is her first book. With Luke Shanahan's help, she combs through nutrition research and draws from her ten-year experience at her practice in Hawaii to compile simple principles for healthy living.

THE END

If you enjoyed this summary, please leave an honest review on Amazon.com…it'd mean a lot to us.

If you haven't already, we encourage you to purchase a copy of the original book.